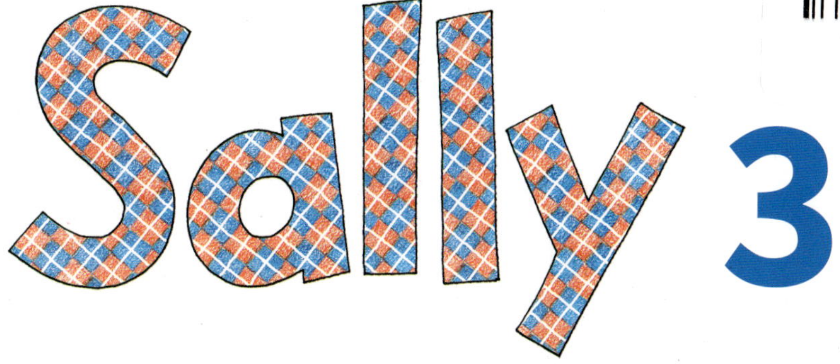

Sally 3

Lehrwerk für den Englischunterricht ab Klasse 3

Pupil's Book 3

Erarbeitet von
Jasmin Brune
Daniela Elsner
Stefanie Gleixner-Weyrauch
Marion Lugauer
Sabine Schwarz

Auf der Grundlage der Ausgabe von
Martina Bredenbröcker, Jasmin Brune,
Daniela Elsner, Barbara Gleich,
Stefanie Gleixner-Weyrauch,
Simone Gutwerk, Marion Lugauer,
Sabine Schwarz, Anke Spangenberg

Unter Beratung von
Jane Brockmann-Fairchild

Illustriert von
Barbara Jung, Wilfried Poll,
Anja Boretzki, Gisela Vogel

Cornelsen

Inhalt

What’s your name?

1 Look and read: My name is …

Susan

Tim

Emily

Phil

Eric

Liz

2 Listen and sing.

Good morning, hello! I am so happy.
Good morning, hello! How are you?

3 Ask your partner: What’s your name? How are you?

English all around

1 **There are many English words in the picture.**
Look and say: I can see …

2 **Which other English words do you know?**

3 **Make a poster with English words.**
Cut out pictures or words from magazines.

★ **Group the words (sports, food, drinks, ...).**

Mr Blue and Mrs Yellow

1 **Listen and point.**

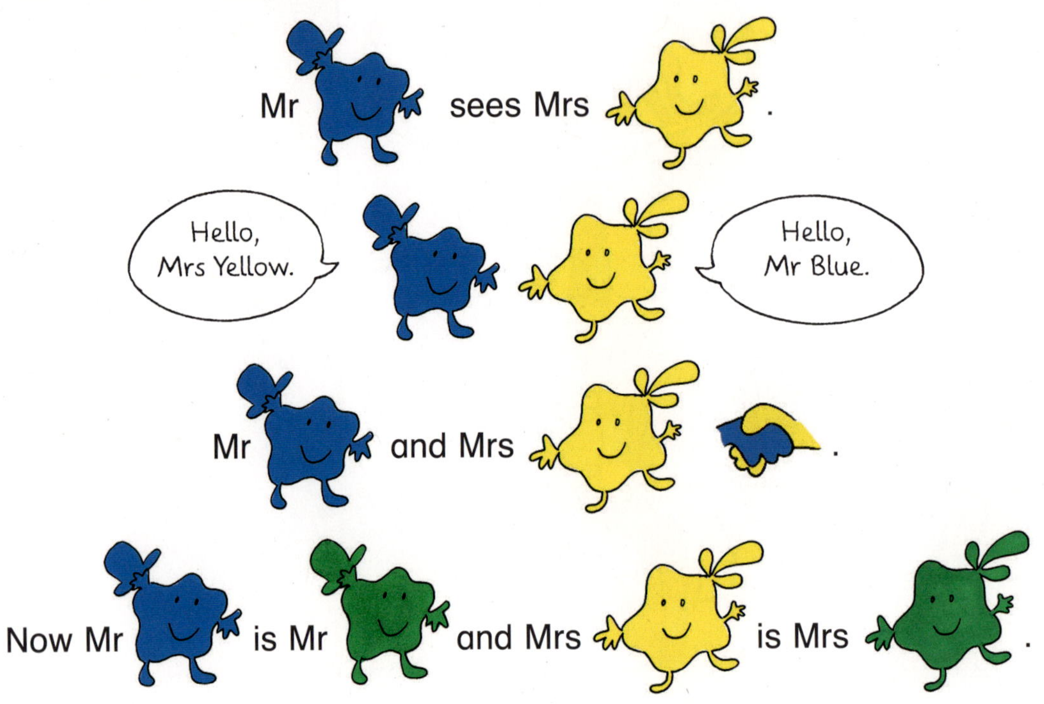

Mr
sees Mrs
.
Hello, Mrs Yellow.
Hello, Mr Blue.
Mr
and Mrs
.
Now Mr
is Mr
and Mrs
is Mrs
.

2 **What colour is it?**

3 **Act out the story with a partner.**

CD 1.4

Sally's rhyme

1 **Listen, say the rhyme and do the actions.**

One, two, three –
Sally, point to me!

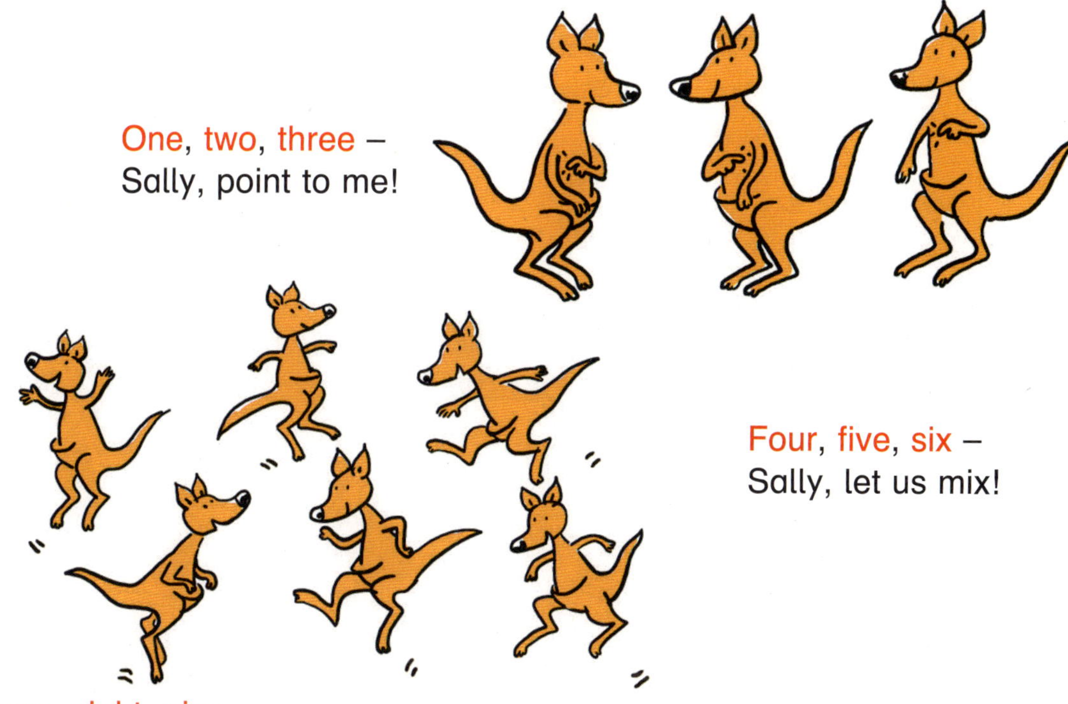

Four, five, six –
Sally, let us mix!

Seven, eight, nine –
now let's stand in line!

Now comes ten,
let's say the rhyme again!

2 **Learn the rhyme.**

CD 1.8

In class

1 **Listen and point.**

2 **What school things have you got?**
Tell your partner: I've got a ...

Make your own picture dictionary. Draw and write.

CD 1.12

School in England

I can see …

In the photo, I can see …

Talk about the photos.

in class

pupils in school uniform

lunchtime

a lollipop lady

Listen and read.

Hello, my name is Ella. I'm 9.
I go to Westminster School. I'm in class 3c.
My teacher is Mrs Black.
My school uniform is red and white.
School starts at 9 o'clock in the morning
and ends at 4 o'clock in the afternoon.
I like music and sports.
What about you?

Make a video.

What about your school day? Do a presentation.

CD 1.15

Head and shoulders

C
G
Head and shoul - ders, knees and toes, knees and toes. Head and
G
C
shoul-ders, knees and toes, knees and toes_ and_ eyes and ears and
F
G7
C F C
mouth and nose, head and shoul-ders, knees and toes, knees and toes.

1 Sing the song and do the actions.

2 Sing the song faster and faster.

3 Sing and drop the word head.
Sing again and drop the words head and shoulders ...

Hm and shoulders, knees ...
Hm and hm, knees ...
one knee – two knees

CD 1.16

Ouch!

1 **Read the comic.**

Good morning, Sally. Here is your tea.

I can't go to school.

Ouch! My ears.

Let me see.

Go to school.

Ouch! My arm.

Let me see.

Go to school.

Ouch! My knee.

Let me see.

Sally, you are okay. Go to school.

2 **Act out the story.**

Snakes and ladders

1 **Play the game. Do the actions.**

FINISH

64	63	**62**	61	60	**59**	**58**	57
49	50	51	**52**	53	54	55	56
48	47	46	45	44	**43**	42	41
33	34	35	36	37	38	39	40
32	31	30	**29**	28	**27**	26	25
17	18	**19**	20	21	22	23	**24**
16	15	14	13	12	11	10	9
1	2	**3**	4	5	6	7	**8**

START

Roll the dice. Do the actions.

 Correct action : Go up the ladder.

Wrong action : Go down the snake.

 Sally's hotspot:

Correct action: Roll the dice again.

Wrong action: Go back to the start.

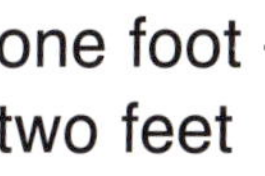

3 Touch your head. 

8 Bend your knees. 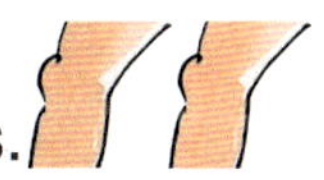

16 Sing: Head and shoulders …

19 Wash your hands. 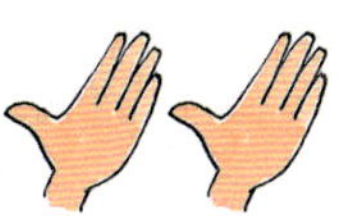

24 Count your fingers. 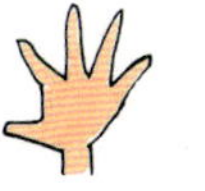

27 Shake your feet. 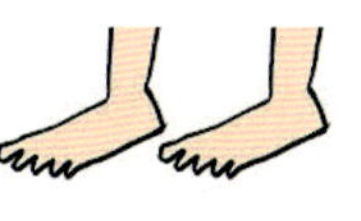

29 Stretch your arms. 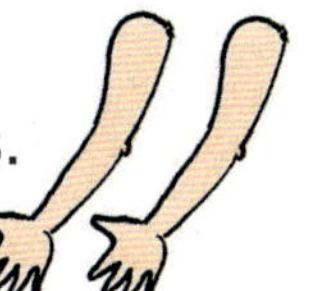

33 Point to your eyes. 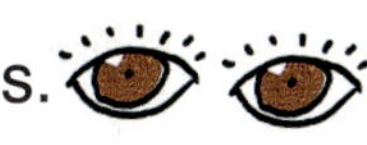

43 Touch your ears. 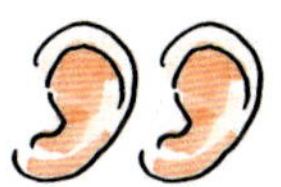

48 Stretch your legs. 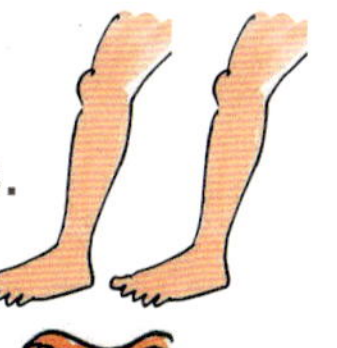

52 Brush your hair. 

58 Say: Good morning!

59 Point to your nose. 

62 Shake your body. 

Monster, monster, how do you feel?

happy

angry

scared

sad

tired

  **Listen, point and say:** The yellow monster is …

  **Draw your own monster and write.**
My monster is …

 **Which emojis do you know? Draw and write.**

Look it up on the Internet.

Tim's wish list

spaceship £17
helicopter £20
helmet £30
bike £90
helmet £40
bike £100 £ 200
castle £80
doll £10
racing car £18
football £8
rubber £1
book £5
ruler £2
pencils £3

1 Look at the toys. What does Tim want? Tell your partner:
Tim wants a bike ...

2 Ask your partner: How much is the ...?

3 Make a wish list for your class and discuss. Use your dictionary.
We want to buy ...

The fish who could wish

In the deep blue sea, in the deep of the blue,
swam a fish who could wish, and each wish would come true.

He wished for a castle.

He wished for a car.

He wished for a horse and a Spanish guitar.

One day, just for fun, that silly old fish,
wished the silliest, silliest wish he could wish.

That silly old fish wished he could be
just like all the other fish in the sea.

But wishing was something other fish could not do.
So that was his very last wish that came true.

1 Listen and point.

2 Look at the pictures.
Tell the story to your partner.

CD 1.23

Sally in the snow

Sally, it's cold!

Sally, it's cold!!!

1 Listen and point.

2 **Look and say:** Sally puts on her … / Sally takes off her …

3 **What are you wearing? Tell your partner:**
I'm wearing …

4 **Do the clothes rally.**

What's the weather like?

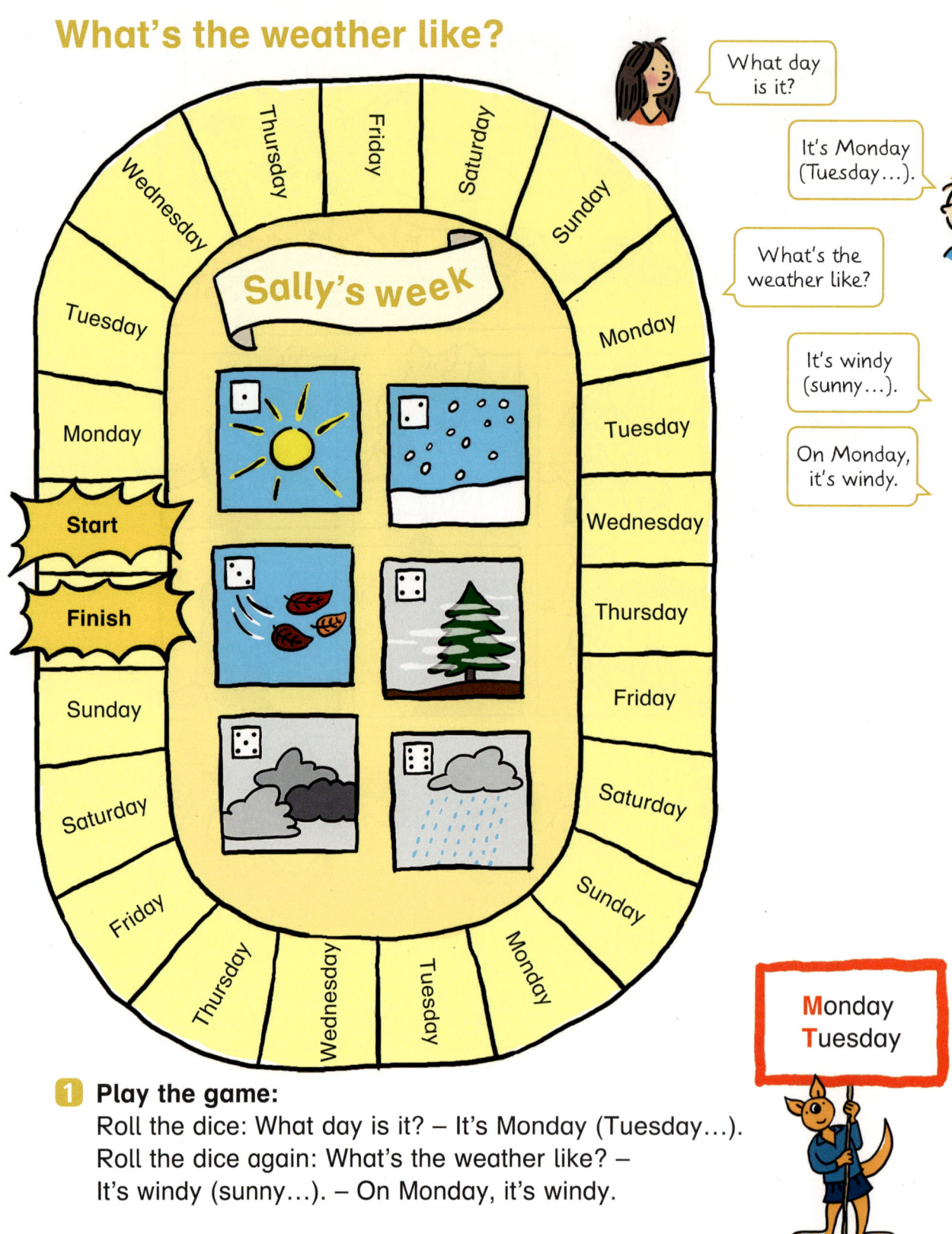

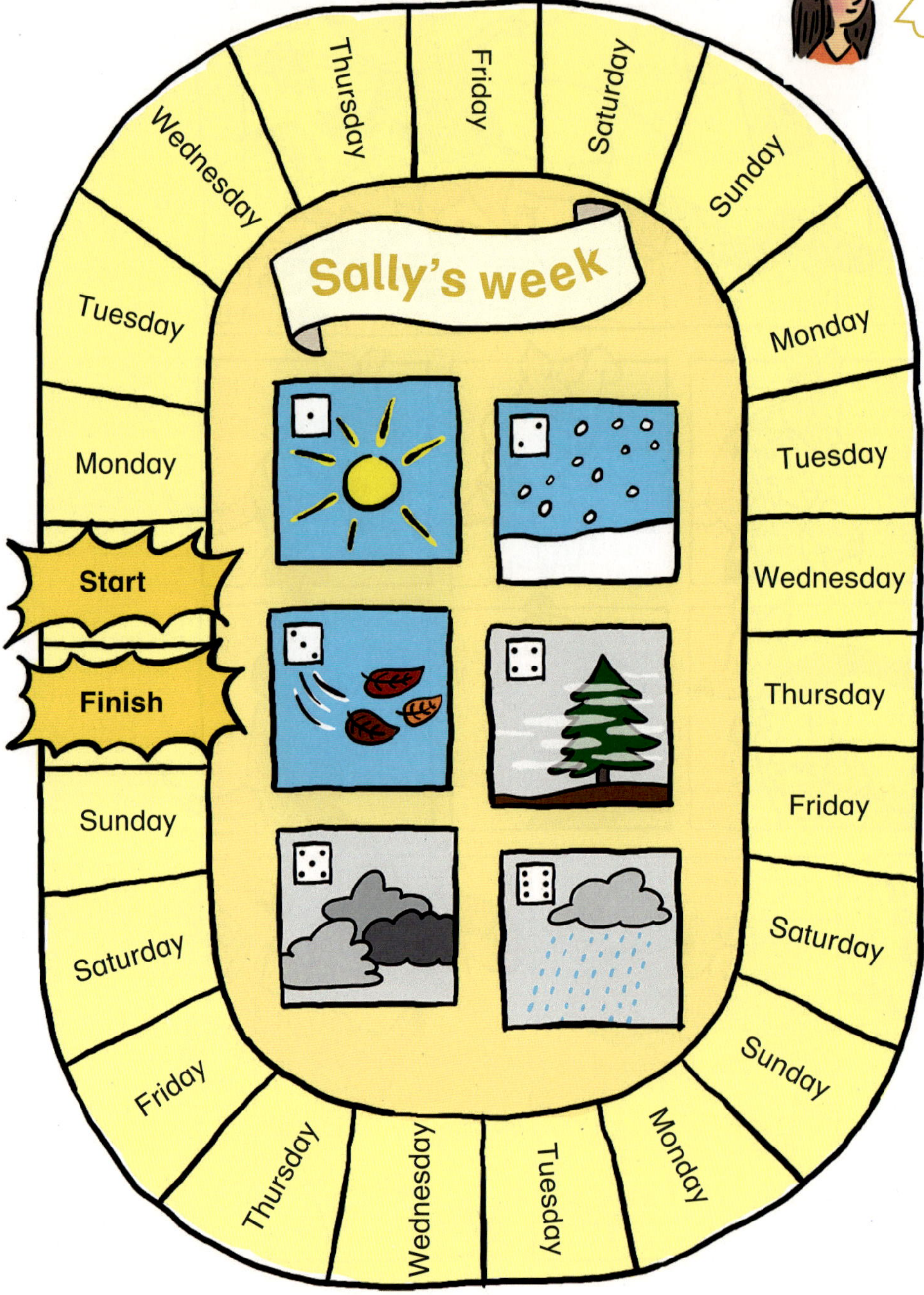

1 Play the game:
Roll the dice: What day is it? – It's Monday (Tuesday…).
Roll the dice again: What's the weather like? –
It's windy (sunny…). – On Monday, it's windy.

The wind and the sun

I'm stronger than you.
I'm stronger than you.

1 Look at the picture. What can you see?

2 Listen to the story. Tell it to your partner.

3 Act out the story in your group.

Make a video.

CD 1.31

The weather forecast

1 **Talk about the picture.**

2 **What's the weather like? Listen, point and tell.**

Look in a newspaper or on the Internet.

3 **What's the weather like in Paris, in Hamburg …? Make a weather forecast in your group and do a presentation.**

Presentation tips:
- Speak loudly and clearly.
- Look at the class.
- Show pictures.

★ **Make a weather chart for one week.**

 CD 1.32

Happy birthday

Birthday invitation

Dear Susan,
Please come to my birthday party.

When: Saturday, 5 March at 2 o'clock
Where: 25, Main Street
Phone: 3472

Can you come to my party?
Yours, Emily

January February March
5 Emily
April May June
July August September
October November December

HAPPY BIRTHDAY

1. Talk about Emily's birthday party.
2. How do you celebrate your birthday? Tell your class.
3. Make a birthday calendar.
4. Write a birthday invitation.

January
February

Keith Haring

the artist

"Best buddies"

"Football"

presentation

1 **Look at the pictures.**
Describe the colours and actions.

friend orange red
blue purple yellow
dance play football

2 **Make a picture about friends:**

1. Cut out different figures.
2. Glue them on coloured paper.
3. Trace your figures with a black pen.

My family

my mum and dad

My brother Tim is 9 years old!

my grandma and grandpa

Can you find my grandma and grandpa?

This is my aunt. Her name is Helen.

Can you find my mum and Tim?

How old is Susan?

1 **Look and point.**

2 **What about your family? Tell:**
I've got … His/her name is … He/She is … years old.

It's magic

Never do magic on your own!

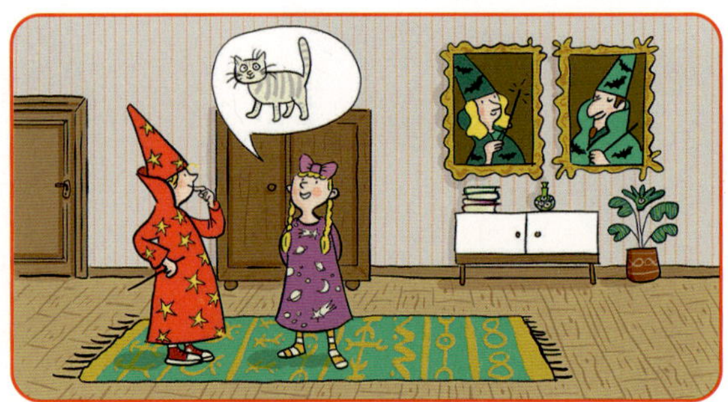

Do magic to get me a cat.

Oh no! Marnie where are you?

Please, help me!

Bubble, bubble, trick and track …

I will never do magic on my own.

1 **Listen and point.**

2 **Act out the story.**

What is it?

tea, coke, orange juice, coffee, hot chocolate, milk

1 Look and guess.

At the drinks stand

What would you like to drink?
I'd like a glass of water, please.
I'm thirsty.

2 Look and read.

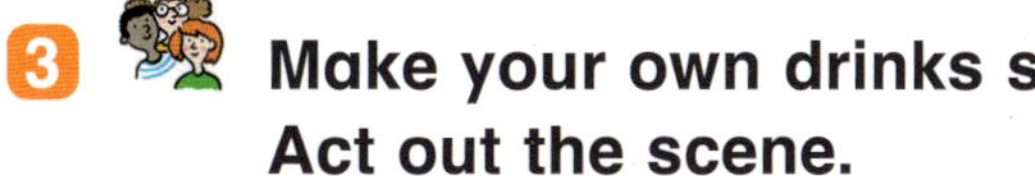

3 Make your own drinks stand. Act out the scene.

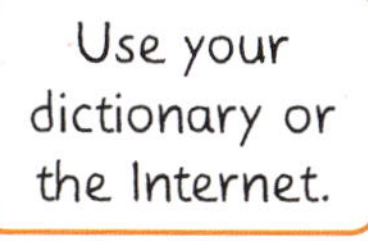
Use your dictionary or the Internet.

4 Make a poster about drinks.

The magic trick

1 Do the trick.

2 Can you do a magic trick? Show your class.

1 orange juice
2 honey
3 tea
4 toast
5 ham
6 water
7 bread
8 hot chocolate
9 jam
10 cheese
11 egg
12 coffee
13 milk
14 roll
15 cornflakes

My favourite breakfast

everyday breakfast

traditional cooked breakfast

1 **Look and speak.**

Do you like
Sugar
on your
in your
CORN FLAKES
?

2 **Ask your partner.**

Do you like …?
Yes, I do.
No, I don't.

3 **What do you have for breakfast?**
For breakfast, I have …

4 **Do the breakfast rally.**

At the ice cream stand

Can I help you?

cherry
banana
pear
vanilla
chocolate
lemon
strawberry
orange
pineapple

Let's have an ice cream.

I'd like …

1 Listen and speak.

2 Make a word web with fruit words. Use your dictionary.

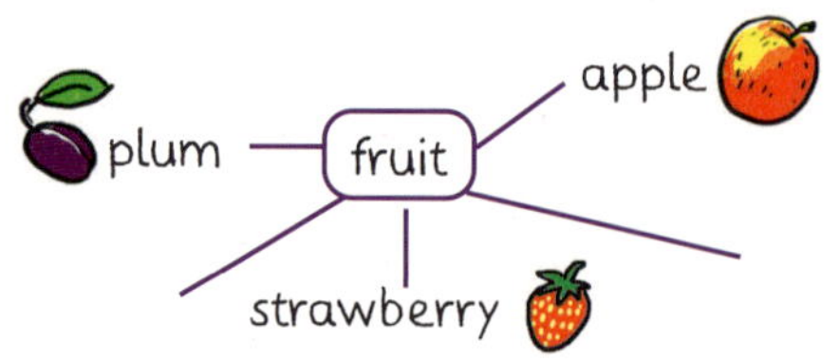

3 Ask your partner:
What's your favourite ice cream?

 CD 1.45

Let's make a smoothie!

1 Look and read.

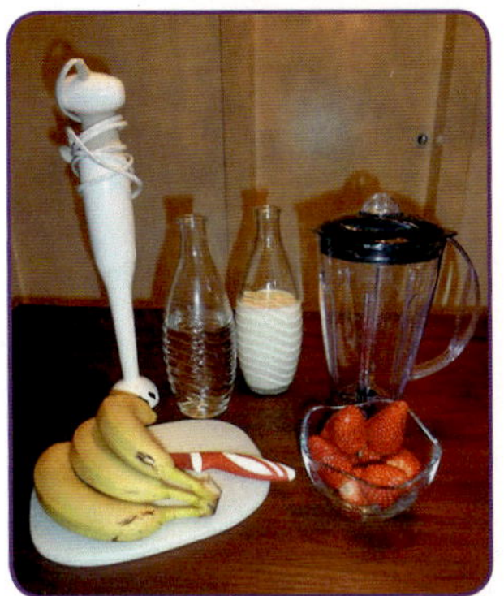

This is what you need.

Wash the strawberries.

Peel the bananas.

Cut the fruit.

Put them into the jug.

Add water or milk.

Mix it.

Pour the smoothie into your glass.

Enjoy!

2  **Make your own smoothie.**

Little dog lost

Listen. Where is Bobby?

These pets have new homes

Jack and Mr Tailor

Tippy and Mrs Davis

Rocky and Sammy Baker

Hopsy and Sophie Miller

Molly and Kevin Fisher

Fred and Alice Smith

Charlie and Mrs Cooper

Speedy

1 **Listen, look and speak.**

2 **Make a missing pet report. Use your dictionary.**

3 **Ask for your pet at the animal centre. Act it out.**

The wheels on the bus

1. The wheels on the bus go round and round,
   round and round, round and round.
   The wheels on the bus go round and round,
   all around the town.

2. The wipers on the bus
   go "Swish, swish, swish" …

3. The horn on the bus goes "Beep, beep, beep" …

4. The driver on the bus says "Move on back!" …

5. The baby on the bus says "Wah, wah, wah!" …

6. The mummy on the bus says "Shh, shh, shh" …

  **Listen, sing and act it out.**

 **Write your own verse. Use your dictionary.**

 CD 2.5

Let's go to London!

the Royal Family

guards

Buckingham Palace

Tower Bridge

the London Eye

Big Ben

Find information on the Internet.

1 **Look at the photos.**

2 **Make a poster about London sights.**

Clumsy the dog

One day at the farm …
Oops!
Clumsy, was that you?
Me? No, it wasn't me.
The next day …
Oops!
Clumsy, was that you?
Me? No, it wasn't me.
The next day …
Oops!
Clumsy, was that you?
Me? No, it wasn't me.

At night ...

The next morning ...

Who stole the eggs?

Clumsy, was that you?

Me? No, it wasn't me. Not this time!

But Clumsy, you always say that.

In the evening ...

CLUMSY

It wasn't me ... Why don't they believe me?

The next morning ...

Wake up! It wasn't Clumsy. Look!

Hold the thief!

Clumsy, good thing you are so clumsy!

Oops!

1 Listen to the story.

2 Read the story.

Alphabet rhyme

A B C D E F G,
on the farm there is a bee.

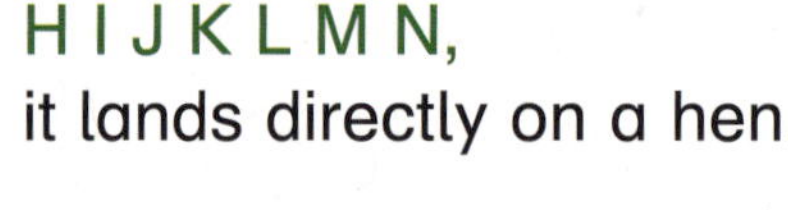

H I J K L M N,
it lands directly on a hen.

O P Q R S T U,
and asks her friendly:
"How are you?"

V W X Y Z,
"I'm fine, but please,
get off my head."

1 **Listen and point.**

2 **Read the rhyme.**

3 **Do the animal rally.**

CD 2.12

I know an old lady ...

1 **Listen and point.**

2 **Read the story:**

I know an old lady who swallowed a fly.
I don't know why she swallowed a fly.

I know an old lady who swallowed a .

.

.

.

She swallowed the  to catch the fly.

 .

 .

 .

I don't know why she swallowed the fly.
I know an old lady who swallowed a horse – and then?
She sneezed, of course!!!

Robin Hood's clever trick

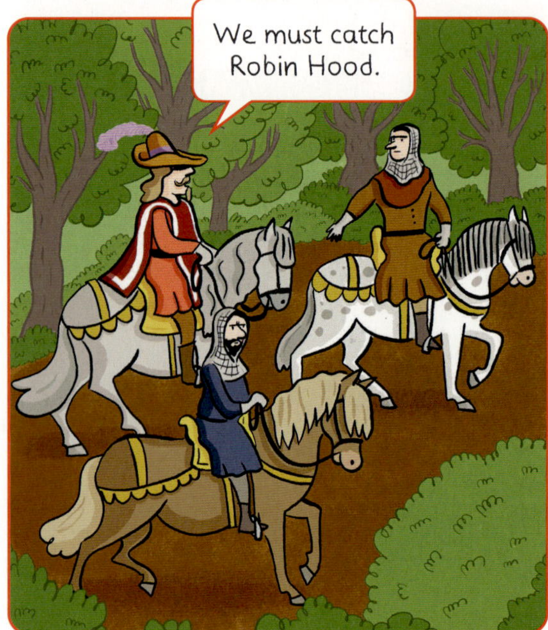

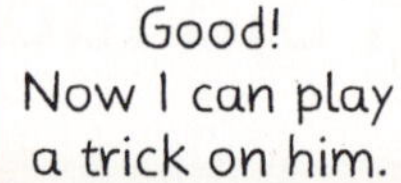

1 **Listen and point.**

2 **Read the story.**

3 **Act out the story.**

Rush hour

The ghost

I saw a ghost.
He saw me, too.
I waved at him.
But he said "Boo!".

Tongue twister

Two witches are watching two watches.
Which witch is watching which watch?

1 Look and read.
Can you say the tongue twister?

Choose a witch and describe her to your partner:
My witch is … Her hair is …

orange | yellow | grey | brown

It's Halloween

What a dark night.

Look, there's Emily's house.

Oh no, there's a bat. I hate bats.

Trick or treat!

Oh no, there's a monster behind the bush. I hate monsters.

1 **Listen to the song.**

2 **Listen to the story.**

★ **Act out the story.**

Christmas Eve

1 Listen to the story.

2 How do you celebrate Christmas?

3 Sing the song. Act it out.

I wish you
a merry Christmas
and a happy New Year.

CD 2.22/2.23

Hurry, Santa!

It is Christmas Eve.
"Hurry, Santa!"

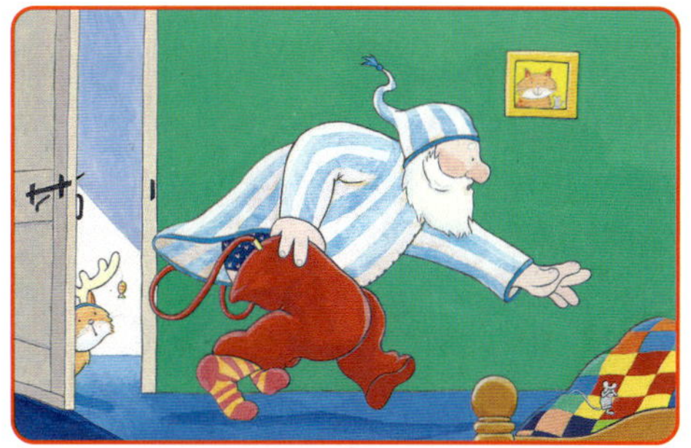

Santa puts on his clothes.

"Go, reindeer, go!"
"Oooooh!" CRASH!

"We did it!" says Santa
back at the North Pole.

"Oh no! I've forgotten someone!"

"That present is for you.
It's Christmas Day!"

1 Listen and point.

2 Read the story.

3 What is Santa's Christmas present? Guess.

Make your own Christmas stocking

You need:
thick brown paper, a pencil, scissors, glue, a hole punch, wool, felt tips or wax crayons and coloured paper

1 Draw a large stocking on the thick brown paper.
2 Cut out two copies of the stocking.

3 Glue the two stockings together around the edges. Leave the top open.

4 Punch holes around the edges of the stocking.
5 Weave wool in and out of the holes.

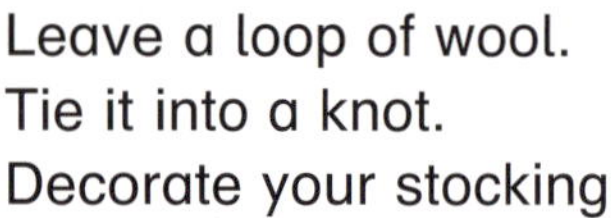

6 Leave a loop of wool. Tie it into a knot. Decorate your stocking.

1 Look and read.

2 Create your own stocking.

Describe your stocking: On my stocking there is/are …

star tree candle

Valentine's cards

1 **Read the comic.**

2 **Read the rhymes. What's your favourite rhyme?**

In February
it's Valentine's Day.
I write Valentine's cards
to my friends.

Jingle, jangle,
silver bangle,
you look fit
from every angle.

Candy is sweet,
this is true,
but for my Valentine
I'll choose you.

I like you!
Be my Valentine!

Roses are red,
violets are blue,
sugar is sweet
and so are you!

3  **Make your own Valentine's card.**

Edgar's Easter eggs

There is …

There are …

1 Talk about the pictures.

I can see …

I like …

2 Listen to the story.

3 Make your own Easter egg cup.

Hello Hallo

boy Junge
girl Mädchen
children Kinder

basketball Basketball
computer game Computerspiel
mobile phone Handy
inline skating Inlineskaten
singing Singen
skateboard Skateboard
tennis Tennis

Hello./Hi. Hallo.

Good morning. Guten Morgen.

How are you? – I'm fine, thanks.
Wie geht es dir? – Danke, gut.

What's your name? – My name is ...
Wie heiβt du? – Ich heiβe ...

What do you like? –
I like ... And you?
Was magst du? –
Ich mag ... Und du?

I can see (a) ... Ich sehe (ein/e) ...

Colours and numbers
Farben und Zahlen

black schwarz
blue blau
brown braun
green grün
grey grau
orange orange
pink rosa, pink
purple lila
red rot
white weiβ
yellow gelb

one eins
two zwei
three drei
four vier
five fünf
six sechs
seven sieben
eight acht
nine neun
ten zehn

What colour is it? –
It's green (blue ...).
Welche Farbe hat es? –
Es ist grün (blau ...).

What's your telephone/mobile number? – My telephone/mobile number is ...
Wie lautet deine Telefonnummer/Handynummer? – Meine Telefonnummer/Handynummer ist ...

At school In der Schule

(black)board Tafel
book Buch
class Klasse
classroom Klassenzimmer
computer Computer
folder Ordner
glue stick Klebestift
lollipop lady Schülerlotsin
pen Füller
pencil Bleistift
pencil case Federmäppchen
pencil sharpener Spitzer

pupil Schüler
rubber Radiergummi
ruler Lineal
school Schule
schoolbag Schultasche
school things Schulsachen
school uniform Schuluniform
(a pair of) scissors eine Schere
teacher Lehrer(in)

in in
on auf
under unter

I've got a … Ich habe ein(e, en) …

I go to Westminster School.
Ich gehe in die Westminster-Schule.

I'm in class 3c.
Ich bin in der Klasse 3c.

My teacher is Mrs/Mr ...
Meine Lehrerin / Mein Lehrer heißt Frau/Herr …

Body and feelings
Körper und Gefühle

arm Arm
body Körper
ear Ohr
eye Auge
face Gesicht
finger Finger
foot – feet Fuß – Füße
hair Haar
hand Hand
head Kopf
knee Knie
leg Bein
mouth Mund
nose Nase
shoulder Schulter
toe Zeh
tooth – teeth Zahn – Zähne

angry zornig
fine gut
happy glücklich
sad traurig
scared verängstigt, erschrocken
tired müde

How do you feel? – I'm happy/sad ...
Wie fühlst du dich? – Ich bin glücklich/traurig …

I'm okay. Mir geht's ganz gut.

Toys Spielzeug

big groß
car Auto
castle Burg, Schloss
children Kinder
computer game Computerspiel
doll Puppe
fish Fisch
football Fußball
guitar Gitarre
helicopter Hubschrauber
helmet Helm
horse Pferd
bike Fahrrad
racing car Rennauto
small klein
spaceship Raumschiff
teddy bear Teddybär
(to) want wollen
(to) wish (for) sich wünschen

eleven elf
twelve zwölf
thirteen dreizehn
fourteen vierzehn
fifteen fünfzehn
sixteen sechzehn
seventeen siebzehn
eighteen achtzehn
nineteen neunzehn
twenty zwanzig

British britisch
money Geld
penny – pence (p) Penny – Pence
pound (£) Pfund

How much is the ...? –
The ... is ... pounds.
Wie viel kostet der (die, das) ...? –
Der (die, das) ... kostet ... Pfund.

How much is it? – It's ... pounds. Wie viel kostet das? – Das macht ... Pfund.

Tim/Susan wants ...
Tim/Susan möchte ...

Clothes Kleidung

boots Stiefel
cap Kappe
coat Mantel
dress Kleid
gloves Handschuhe
jacket Jacke
(a pair of) jeans eine Jeans
pullover Pullover
(to) put on anziehen
scarf Schal
shirt Hemd
shoes Schuhe
(a pair of) shorts
eine kurze Hose, Shorts
skirt Rock
socks Socken
(to) take off ausziehen
(a pair of) trousers eine Hose
T-shirt T-Shirt
(to) wear tragen, anhaben
woolly hat Mütze

For my holidays, I pack ...
Für meine Ferien packe ich ... ein.

Sally puts on her ... / takes off her ...
Sally zieht ihr(e, en) ... an/aus.

Weather and days
Wetter und Tage

Monday Montag
Tuesday Dienstag
Wednesday Mittwoch
Thursday Donnerstag
Friday Freitag
Saturday Samstag
Sunday Sonntag
day Tag
week Woche

cloud/y Wolke/wolkig
cold kalt
fog/gy Nebel/neblig
hot heiß
rain/y Regen/regnerisch
snow/y Schnee/verschneit
sun/ny Sonne/sonnig
weather forecast Wettervorhersage
wind/y Wind/windig

When can we meet? – We can meet on Monday (Tuesday …). Wann können wir uns treffen? – Wir können uns am Montag (Dienstag …) treffen.

What day is it? – It's Monday. (Tuesday ...). Welchen Tag haben wir? – Es ist Montag (Dienstag ...).

What's the weather like today? – Today it's windy (sunny …).
Wie ist das Wetter heute? –
Heute ist es windig (sonnig …).

On Monday, it's sunny.
Am Montag ist es sonnig.

Around the year
Rund ums Jahr

January Januar
February Februar
March März
April April
May Mai
June Juni
July Juli
August August
September September
October Oktober
November November
December Dezember
month Monat

spring Frühling
summer Sommer
autumn Herbst
winter Winter
season Jahreszeit

balloon Ballon
birthday Geburtstag
cake Torte, Kuchen
calendar Kalender
candle Kerze
card Karte
crown Krone
guest Gast
invitation Einladung
party Party, Feier
present Geschenk

When's your birthday? –
My birthday is in …
Wann ist dein Geburtstag? –
Mein Geburtstag ist im …

Happy birthday!
Alles Gute zum Geburtstag!

How old are you? – I'm eight (years old).
Wie alt bist du? –
Ich bin acht (Jahre alt).

Family and friends
Familie und Freunde

aunt Tante
boy Junge
brother Bruder
family Familie
father/dad Vater/Papa
friend Freund(in)
girl Mädchen
grandfather/grandpa Großvater/Opa
grandmother/grandma
Großmutter/Oma
mother/mum Mutter/Mama
sister Schwester
uncle Onkel

My best friend is ...
Mein(e) beste(r) Freund(in) ist ...

He/She is ... years old.
Er/Sie ist ... Jahre alt.

He/She has got ... Er/Sie hat ...

Have you got brothers or sisters? –
I've got ... / I haven't got ...
Hast du Geschwister? –
Ich habe ... / Ich habe keine ...

This is my family. /
These are my friends.
Das ist meine Familie. /
Dies sind meine Freunde.

Drinks Getränke

coffee Kaffee
coke Cola
hot chocolate Kakao
lemonade Limonade
(a glass of) milk (ein Glas) Milch
orange juice Orangensaft
(a cup of) tea (eine Tasse) Tee
water Wasser

What drinks do you like? – I like ...
Welche Getränke magst du? –
Ich mag ...

I like ... best. Am liebsten mag ich ...

What drinks don't you like? –
I don't like ...
Welche Getränke magst du nicht? –
Ich mag kein(e, en) ...

What would you like to drink? –
I'd like ..., please. Was würdest du gerne trinken? – Ich hätte gerne ..., bitte.

Breakfast Frühstück

bread Brot
breakfast Frühstück
butter Butter
cheese Käse
cornflakes Cornflakes
(to) drink trinken
(to) eat essen
egg Ei
ham Schinken
honey Honig
jam Marmelade
roll Brötchen
toast Toast

What do you have for breakfast?
Was isst/trinkst du zum Frühstück?

For breakfast, I have ...
Zum Frühstück esse/trinke ich ...

Do you like ...? –
Yes, I do. / No, I don't.
Magst du ...? – Ja. / Nein.

Can I have the ..., please? –
Here you are. Kann ich bitte den/die/das ... haben? – Hier, bitte.

Fruit Obst

apple Apfel
banana Banane
cherry Kirsche
fruit Frucht, Obst
lemon Zitrone
melon Melone
orange Orange, Apfelsine
pear Birne

pineapple Ananas
plum Pflaume
strawberry Erdbeere
tree Baum

(to) add hinzufügen
(to) cut schneiden
ice cream Eiskrem
ice cream stand Eisstand
jug Krug
(to) mix mischen
(to) peel schälen
(to) pour eingießen
(to) put hineingeben, legen, stellen
scoop Eiskugel
smoothie Smoothie, Fruchtshake
(to) wash waschen

What's your favourite ice cream?
Was ist dein Lieblingseis?

Can I help you?
Kann ich dir/euch/Ihnen helfen?

I'd like … – Here you are.
Ich hätte gerne … – Hier, bitte.

That's … pounds, please. – Thank you.
Das macht bitte … Pfund. – Danke.

Goodbye. Auf Wiedersehen.

Pets Haustiere

bird Vogel
budgie Wellensittich
cat Katze
dog Hund
fish Fisch(e)
guinea pig Meerschweinchen
hamster Hamster
mouse – mice Maus – Mäuse
pet Haustier
rabbit Kaninchen
tail Schwanz
tortoise Schildkröte
wing Flügel

What's your favourite pet?
Was ist dein Lieblingshaustier?

My favourite pet is a …
Mein Lieblingshaustier ist ein(e) …

Its name is … Es heißt …

Can I help you? – I've lost my pet.
Kann ich dir/euch/Ihnen helfen? – Ich habe mein Haustier verloren.

What colour is it? – It's black (brown …).
Welche Farbe hat es? – Es ist schwarz (braun …).

London London

bus Bus
bus driver Busfahrer
England England
guard Wache, Wachposten
king König
(to) move bewegen, sich bewegen
palace Palast
prince Prinz
princess Prinzessin
queen Königin
Royal Family Königsfamilie
sight Sehenswürdigkeit

I want to be a … Ich will ein(e) … sein.

I want to see … Ich will … sehen.

Farm animals
Bauernhoftiere

animal Tier
barn Stall
bee Biene
clumsy ungeschickt
cow Kuh
duck Ente
farm Bauernhof
farmer Bauer
goose – geese Gans – Gänse
hen Huhn, Henne
horse Pferd
pig Schwein
sheep Schaf, Schafe

What's your favourite animal? –
It's a …
Was ist dein Lieblingstier? –
Es ist ein(e) …

Robin Hood Robin Hood

arrow Pfeil
bow Bogen
castle Burg, Schloss
(to) catch fangen
(to) dress up sich verkleiden
forest Wald
hat Hut
(to) play a trick
einen Streich spielen
poor arm
rich reich
(to) ride (a horse)
(ein Pferd) reiten
sheriff Sheriff
(to) shoot schießen

Help! Hilfe!

Hands up! Hände hoch!

Happy Halloween
Fröhliches Halloween

bat Fledermaus
broom Besen
costume Kostüm, Verkleidung
dark dunkel
door Tür
ghost Geist, Gespenst
Halloween Halloween
hat Hut
house Haus
(to) knock klopfen
monster Ungeheuer, Monster
moon Mond
night Nacht
pumpkin Kürbis
(to) shake schütteln
skeleton Gerippe, Skelett
star Stern
sweets Süßigkeiten
witch Hexe

Happy Halloween!
Fröhliches Halloween!

It's eight (nine …) o'clock.
Es ist acht (neun …) Uhr.

Trick or treat!
Süßes oder Saures!

Words

Merry Christmas
Frohe Weihnachten

bell Glocke
carrot Karotte
chimney Schornstein
Christmas card Weihnachtskarte
Christmas Eve Heiligabend, Weihnachtsabend
Christmas tree Weihnachtsbaum
Father Christmas Weihnachtsmann
fireplace (offener) Kamin
(to) get presents Geschenke bekommen
hungry hungrig
mistletoe Mistel(zweig)
reindeer Rentier(e)
sleigh Schlitten
snowman Schneemann
stocking Strumpf

Merry Christmas! Frohe Weihnachten!

I wish you a happy New Year!
Ich wünsche dir ein frohes neues Jahr!

Valentine's Day
Valentinstag

Valentine's Day Valentinstag

(to) write Valentine's cards
Valentinskarten schreiben

It's Valentine's Day.
Es ist Valentinstag.

I like you. Ich mag dich.

Happy Easter Frohe Ostern

basket Korb
bush Busch
(to) colour färben, anmalen
Easter bunny Osterhase
Easter egg Osterei
Easter egg cup Ostereierbecher
fence Zaun
fun Spaß
happy glücklich
(to) hide verstecken
sad traurig
(to) share teilen

behind hinter
in in
in front of vor
on auf
under unter

Happy Easter! Frohe Ostern!

Is the yellow (red ...) egg in/on/under the ...?
Ist das gelbe (rote ...) Ei in/auf/unter dem/der ...?